What is a Forest?

Forests are environments where trees are the main plants. There are three types of forest – tropical, **temperate** and **boreal**.

The type of forest that grows depends mainly on the **climate**.

Tropical forests grow near the **Equator**. They can be dry or wet. Wet tropical forests are called rainforests. Most trees in rainforests are evergreen. This means they have leaves all year round.

Temperate forests grow where there are big changes in the weather from season to season. There is a cold winter, a warm summer and lots of rain. Many temperate forests have **deciduous** trees. This means they lose leaves in autumn and grow new ones in spring.

Boreal forests grow in the cold, northern parts of the world. This is where there are short summers and long, dry winters. **Conifers** are the most common trees in boreal forests.

Forests

Forests

contents

Copyright © 2007 Blake Publishing
Additional material © A & C Black Publishers Ltd 2008

First published in Australia by Blake Education Pty Ltd

This edition published in the UK in 2008 by
A & C Black Publishers Ltd, 38 Soho Square, London. W1D 3HB
www.acblack.com

Published by permission of Blake Publishing Pty Ltd, Leichhardt NSW, Australia.

Hardback edition
ISBN 978-1-4081-0485-9

Paperback edition
ISBN 978-1-4081-0484-2

A CIP record for this book is available from the British Library.

Author: Ian Rohr
Publisher: Katy Pike
Editor: Mark Stafford
Design and layout by The Modern Art Production Group

Image credits: p9 Illustrations – Toby Quarmby
Printed in China by WKT Company Ltd.

Temperate forests are more open than tropical or boreal forests.

Boreal forests are also called taiga forests.

GO FACT!

THE OLDEST
The world's oldest living thing is a conifer.

Rainforests contain many ferns and mosses.

5

Forests of the World

A forest is often dominated by a few types of tree.

Tropical rainforests contain trees with large leaves. The tallest trees form a top layer called a **canopy**. The canopy stops most of the sunlight from reaching the ground. Shorter trees grow between the canopy and the ground.

Some temperate forests contain deciduous trees with broad leaves, such as oak, birch, ash and maple trees. **Eucalypts** are the main trees in Australian temperate forests. Sometimes, there will only be one **species** of tree in a temperate forest, but usually there is a mixture of three or four.

Boreal forests have conifers, such as pine, spruce and fir trees. Conifers have waxy, needle-like leaves. These leaves reduce the loss of heat and water from the trees.

There are more than 700 species of eucalypts.

DID YOU KNOW?

A rainforest might have more than 100 different tree species in a square kilometre.

Forests are great places for camping and hiking.

Deciduous trees do not grow during winter.

Forests cover almost one-third of the Earth's land.

The boreal forests in Siberia make up the largest forest region. They cover almost four million square kilometres.

The Amazon rainforest is shrinking every day. People cut and burn down trees for wood products and to clear the land for farms. Most of the temperate forests that once covered Europe and North America have already been cleared.

GO FACT!

DID YOU KNOW?
Trees produce the oxygen we need to breathe.

Winter lasts at least six months in the Siberian forests.

World forests about 8000 years ago

World forests today

9

Forest Plants

Mosses, wildflowers, vines and ferns grow beneath the forest canopy.

When a tree in the forest dies, it falls to the ground and begins to rot. This tree provides food for other plants. Fallen trees open up the canopy and let more light in for the plants below.

Epiphytes are common in forests. These are plants that grow on other plants instead of in soil. They live attached to a trunk or branch. Epiphytes get most of their food and water from the air. Some epiphytes have leaves that are shaped to catch the rain. Up to half of the plants in tropical rainforests are epiphytes.

Vines use trees to support them as they grow.

THE LARGEST

Some orchids are epiphytes.
They are the largest group of
flowering plants in the world,
with more than 20 000 species.

Ferns like wet conditions
on the forest floor.

Bushfires cause some eucalypts
to produce new seeds.

Mosses grow in damp areas.

Forest Animals

Forests are full of animals.

There are more insects in a forest than any other type of animal. They make up half the mass of all animal life in a rainforest.

About half of all the world's animal species live in tropical rainforests. Hundreds of bird, mammal and reptile species live in each square kilometre of tropical rainforest.

Most rainforest mammals and reptiles are **arboreal**. This means they spend most of their lives in the trees.

Tigers blend in with the forest.

Small animals, such as possums, are common in temperate forests.

There are fewer animals in the cold, boreal forests than in tropical and temperate forests. Some species, such as squirrels, store food to eat in winter.

Cockatoos nest inside hollow tree trunks.

Monkeys use their tails to balance in the trees.

Sloths spend nearly all their lives in rainforest trees.

13

Forest Food Chain

A food chain shows how each living thing gets its food. In a forest, some animals eat plants, and some animals eat other animals.

1. Trees and other plants are the beginning of food chains. They make their own food using the energy of the Sun.

2. Plant eaters feed on shoots, leaves, fruits, nuts and berries.

3. **Predators** hunt plant eaters and smaller predators. When predators die, they are eaten by other animals or they rot into the ground. This helps plants to grow, so the food chain continues.

The green tree python is a rainforest predator.

New birch leaves

Grey wolves

Elk

The Amazon Rainforest

The Amazon rainforest is the largest tropical rainforest on Earth.

It is a hot and wet place. The temperature rarely drops below 22 °C (71.6 °F). The annual rainfall is more than two metres.

Tall trees grow close together and form a thick canopy. Below the canopy is a layer of shorter trees and plants. The ground is covered with twigs and leaves.

Some frogs in the Amazon produce poison on their backs.

Most larger animals live in the rainforest's canopy. This is where there are fruits, seeds and other animals to eat.

Thousands of small rivers flow through the Amazon rainforest into the huge Amazon River. The area covered by these rivers triples during the rainy season.

The wings of the blue morpho butterfly are 15 centimetres wide.

The Amazon rainforest has more animal and plant species than any other forest.

THE HEAVIEST

The world's heaviest snake, the anaconda, lives in the Amazon rainforest.

Macaws are the largest parrots in the world.

Forest plants contain chemicals that can be made into medicines.

Plants make these chemicals to protect themselves from diseases, pests and plant eaters.

People living in forests make medicines from plants. They use seeds, leaves, fruits and bark.

Scientists also make medicines from forest plants. The medicines are used to treat cancer, asthma and many other diseases. The drug Taxol, which is used to treat cancer, comes from the bark of the Pacific yew tree.

A nightshade

The family of nightshade plants is used in different ways. Some types of nightshades, such as potatoes, can be eaten. Other types, such as belladonna, are poisonous. Some of the poisonous plants can be made into medicines.

The annatto tree is used to treat burns and headaches.

GO FACT!

THE SMELLIEST

The smelliest plant on Earth is a corpse flower, discovered in an Indonesian rainforest. Its giant flowers smell like rotting meat.

Medicines made from foxgloves help with heart problems.

The oil in eucalypt leaves can relieve coughs and colds.

How Old is This Tree?

A tree gets bigger every year by adding a new layer of growth.

Trees grow fastest in spring but stop growing in winter. This pattern of growth produces a growth ring in the trunk.

The growth ring is wide when there has been lots of rain during the year. When the year has been dry, the growth ring is narrow.

If you cut the tree in half, you can count the number of rings. This tells you how old the tree is. If there are 70 rings, for example, the tree is 70 years old.

You don't need to cut a tree down to measure how old it is. You can also drill into the tree and remove a piece of the trunk to count the layers of growth. This doesn't kill the tree.

The tree's newest growth ring is under the bark.

A dark line shows when the tree stopped growing in winter.

This is a wide ring from a wet year.

Bristlecone pines can live for thousands of years.

Tree rings can show the age of old furniture.

	Evergreen	Deciduous
Summer		
Autumn		
Winter		
Spring		

Glossary

arboreal	living in trees
boreal	a type of forest in the northern parts of the world
canopy	the top layer of branches in a forest
climate	the typical weather of a place
conifer	an evergreen tree with seeds in cones
deciduous	a tree that loses its leaves in autumn and grows new ones in spring
epiphyte	a plant that gets water and food from the air and rain
Equator	an imaginary line drawn around the middle of the Earth, halfway between the North and South Poles
eucalypt	a type of evergreen Australian tree
predator	an animal that hunts, kills and eats other animals
species	a set of animals or plants in which the members look the same
temperate	a type of forest in a mild climate

Index